Autism and Toilet Training Made Easier

Professional, Realistic, and Positive Advice for Parents with a Child with Autism, or another Developmental or Intellectual Disability

Written by **Trevor Lewis** PGDipSci (Psych), BA (Psych)
Behaviour Specialist

First Published December 2013
Dunedin, New Zealand

Copyright Trevor Lewis, Dunedin, New Zealand
December 2013

About the author

My name is Trevor Lewis, and I am a New Zealand based Behaviour Specialist. Human Sciences has been my interest and my career for over 12 years now, with nearly ten of those specifically in specialist behaviour support services for families with a family member who has a diagnosis of autism, Aspergers, an intellectual disability, or another developmental disability and severely challenging behaviour.

My educational background consists of eight years of study in Psychology, human behaviour, Forensic Psychiatry, addiction studies and other human sciences.

I have written two books on behaviour modification, and a booklet on Toilet Training in addition to this booklet. I have also designed Social Skills Games, a behaviour modification course for people interested in behavioural sciences, a children's anger management program, and other specialist resources.

If I had to sum up my attitude to behaviour modification it would be 'Go back to the basics, and start again'. Find the function of the behaviour, what is reinforcing it, and devise your strategy from there. Oh, and never give up – that is one thing any human can do for free, never give up.'

I live with my beautiful Wife Di, and three of my children in the beautiful first city of New Zealand, Dunedin, which was recently voted 'Best City in New Zealand to Live In'.

COPYRIGHT ©

The full contents of this booklet are copyright to Trevor Lewis, Dunedin, New Zealand. December 2013.

Any distribution or copying of this booklet without the express permission of the author will result in legal action being taken to the full extent of the law.

ISBN 978-1494843496

Forward

I have spent nearly ten years supporting Parents with specialist behavioural advice for their child or adult family member who had Autism, Aspergers, or another developmental or intellectual disability. During that time a large percentage of those I supported either requested that I also help them with toilet training their child or I suggested that one of the behaviour related issues we deal with was to get their child toilet trained.

Unfortunately one of the biggest issues I have come across that either hinders or completely stops progress in toilet training, is well meaning others, or even some "Health Professionals" giving very unhelpful advice, or even telling Parents they just should not worry about their child using the toilet "After all, they have a disability" is what some were told!

Though there are a tiny fraction of people, due to the severity of their disability or other factors that make learning to toilet train very difficult or not practical, I have found almost every child that I have helped a Parent with in regards to toileting strategies have been toilet trained to 100% success, or very close to it. My previous toileting booklet (which contains strategies that some of those in this booklet are based on), "Toilet Training Using the Dior Method" has sold well over 3000 copies in the last few years. From all the feedback I have received, at least 99% of those who were consistent and persistent in following through with my strategies achieved success, many within just a few days!

This new booklet, 'Autism and Toilet Training', details my strategies with a focus on the different needs of children with Autism or an intellectual disability (I.D.).

One of my main pieces of advice to Parents and other people who support a child with a disability such as autism or I.D., is forget what you have been told before, do not be distracted by others who usually mean well but may not be helpful in you achieving success. Follow my strategies as close as you can, and ensure you have consistency, and don't give up! If you have been consistent, and others who support your child have also been consistent in following the strategies for at least ten days, and you have had no success, give it a break for say three or four weeks, then try again, and ensure 100% consistency, re-read the strategies and make sure you are following them as close as possible.

My successes include having children who have never had a bowel motion into a toilet for their first ten years of life, doing their 'poos' into the toilet within days of their Parents implementing my strategies, and being almost 100% consistent with their toileting every time every day within 4 to 5 weeks. I have also seen children who rarely used the toilet for 'wees' or 'poos' for nine years, using the toilet regularly every day within two weeks of following through with my strategies.

Though of course every child is an individual, and I can not guarantee success, I do encourage you to give this booklet a good read, and give the strategies a go. Staying positive and strong despite the odd accident or lack of early success usually reaps rewards. If not, you can at least say you tried the best, and now you need to have another think about what you may need to do.

Best of luck, stay positive!

Trevor Lewis

INDEX

- -7- Need to know terms
- -8- Basics about autism and toilet training
- -15- Important issues
- -17- Autism / Intellectual Disability specific nappy issues
- -22- Strategy one – The Dior Method
- -32- Strategy two – Sit and Wait
- -38- Strategy three – Fixed Scheduling
- -44- Night time tips
- -50- Poo's in the loo
- -57- Desensitisation
- -61- Gaining Compliance

Need to Know Terms

Void – to rid oneself of waste either by urination or by bowel motion.

Positive reinforcer – a reinforcer is something special that the child enjoys having access to (special toy, book, music, drink). Naturally one for the toilet should be something that can be kept there hygienically.

Positively reinforce – reward the individual in a way that they will feel good.
This may be saying well done, it may be access to a special toy, or a special snack

Secondary Reinforcer – a reinforcer (treat) that is in addition to verbal praise

Cue – A hint, sign or indication

Generalise – to take the behaviour into other environments, other times, for other people

Hand-over-hand prompting – placing your hand lightly on the hand or arm of the person being trained, and gently guiding their motions to achieve the task being taught.

Fading – slowly reducing the amount of reinforcers supplied or prompts given

Basics about Autism and Toilet Training

There are a few specific things that people who are about to embark on the 'toilet training mission' with a child with autism need to keep in mind. I have outlined what I think are the main issues below, but first a general summary of problems I have found parents usually encounter when first starting.

First of all, I have found that Parents usually try and delay the toilet training process, and then delay it some more, and some more. Though I can completely understand how this happens when there are often so many other issues being worked on, or that need to be worked on, having a toilet trained child usually makes many other day to day activities that little bit easier and that little bit less stressful. So, I advise you do put toilet training to near the top of your list of what you want to achieve in the near future, but also ensure you choose a time to start when you feel you have the energy, patience, and can ensure consistency. But, don't start using the "I will do it in the holidays, or maybe the next holidays after that, or…" excuse and again find that you are just delaying doing it.

As I have already mentioned some well meaning others, including some "Health Professionals" sometimes give out advice which I have found to be less than helpful, and in some cases made toilet training even harder or more stressful than it needed to be. Some of the advice I believe you should definitely avoid following is:

1) ***Using non-relevant visuals.*** People with autism are very concrete in their thinking, so when using visuals to help teach a behaviour they need to be visuals that relate directly to what it is being taught. In toileting these are likely to be visuals of the toilet/bathroom, toilet paper, washing hands, etc. I have seen people given visuals and/or social stories that included pictures of a dog pooing outside, a cat using a litter tray, etc. Talk about giving out confusing information! Here we are trying to encourage and teach our child to use the toilet, and only toilet inside, but here are visuals of animals being allowed to toilet anywhere but the toilet. Plus the mere detail that our child isn't an animal!

2) ***Encouraging use of nappies, rather than getting rid of them.*** Nappies have one function, to contain wees and poos. So if we are on one hand telling our child we want them to use the toilet, then on the other putting them in a nappy which is for, yes you guessed it, going to toilet in, a child with autism really starts to wonder what message we are trying to give them.

3) ***No sense of purpose to what is to be achieved.*** Parents are also sometimes told to 'not rush it, just

do a little here, and a little there'. Or even worse, 'they will pick it up by themselves when they are ready'. Though of course we do not want our child to become very stressed or overly anxious, we want to achieve toilet training like we would want to achieve any other new skill, as quickly as possible within reason, and more importantly successfully. I believe if you set a specific goal to achieve toilet training, and plan accordingly to achieve that goal in a set time, you will be more than likely to achieve it if you follow the strategies you decided on in this booklet. As you will agree, having purpose and meaning in what we do is an important part of life. Your child will also be more likely to succeed if he or she is focussed on learning this new behaviour and making it habit over a fairly short set period of time, because if you do a little here and a little there, they are more likely to get confused or frustrated in regards to understanding what it is you want them to do.

Now we need to look at other important aspects of toilet training that are very relevant to children with autism, and many with an intellectual disability.

Loss of routine: Children with autism often live their lives through routines that they have formed, or adjusted to. So, changing from voiding in a nappy, to now being expected to sit on a plastic or wooden seat with a hole in it, is a frightening experience. Often the routines they have developed have given them a sense of control over what is otherwise a chaotic and frightening World full of movements, noises, colours and smells. For this reason, using desensitisation methods, and getting them used to the changes more slowly may help. This does mean some extra work beforehand may be needed to get success with the strategies suggested. In fact studies trialling strategies similar to mine have shown that even severely autistic children can be toilet trained within days.

It is not uncommon for a child with autism to be around four or five years of age, or sometimes even older before Parents start tackling the toileting issue, so do not feel guilty or isolated if your child is around this age.

Concrete Thinking: If it is black and white, it is black and white – not white and black. This type of thinking is common in autism. What you see, is what it is. So, if I poo in the toilet bowl, I need to know this is what is supposed to happen to my poos. That is, we need to make it clear that this behaviour is correct, good, and positive. Ensure they see others in the household using the toilet, if possible let them watch a member of the same sex go through the whole process (yes a little uncomfortable for some I know, but it may be very helpful particularly for some with autism).

However, empathic understanding lacks in many people with autism. That is, they have difficulty seeing others points of view – or even accepting that others have feelings, and so just because someone else does their poos and wees in the toilet, doesn't mean they should. **So – using visuals may help overcome this issue**.

Visuals: What I would recommend is having their photo, at the top of a card, followed by sketches of a person weeing and pooing ('boardmaker' type visuals may be useful here), then a photo of your toilet bowl, all with a smiley face or tick next to them. Depending on your child's current level of understanding (their level of intellectual disability) let them know the 'rule is, all wees and poos go in the toilet'. You may need to repeat this 'rule' dozens of times over a period of weeks to really get the message across, but once they have understood and accepted this rule, you will find in almost all cases they stick to it like glue! However, keep in mind this is just one helpful addition to the training process, and not a 'one off' strategy that will achieve toileting by itself.

What happens, how does it work? With autism comes what could be termed, a natural curiosity of how things work. This may be related to their need to have some sort of control over the chaotic World around them. So, talking about (and using pictures) of 'where your poos go' once they are flushed, may be helpful. Show a picture of the toilet bowl, the pipe going from the toilet bowl to the main sewage pipe, and some sort of representation of the sewerage plant. Show, and explain, how their poos in the toilet go down the pipe, into the big pipe, and to the sewer where they turn to dirt (or whatever more imaginative description you can come up with). Though some affected by autism are affected to such an extent they may not be able to understand these concepts, others who can may find this very helpful.

Generalise: As people with autism are very rule based in their behaviour, governed by routine and structure, you need to be extra careful about generalising what is being taught. In other words, **introduce other toilets in other environments early in the training process**. Use other support people and family members in the training. Differ times, clothing worn, and route you take to the toilet (where applicable) so your child does not just toilet appropriately for one person, or only in one environment, or only during the daytime or evening, etc. If you stick to a specific routine (same person, same training times, etc) you may well find they will also stick to these, as this has become the set toileting routine.

Note: The strategies described in this book are for both males and females. I sometimes use the term 'her/she' or 'him/he', but these are not an indication that the strategy is only for a female or only a male, it's more so just to help with grammatical flow.

Toilet training could be one of the most stressful events parents and children go through in the early years. Yet it need not be a drawn out issue, and in many cases – even with developmentally delayed children, can be resolved within a week, and sometimes less.

The three strategies outlined in this book have been adapted specifically to meet the needs of children with autism, an intellectual or developmental disability.
Parents of neuro-typical children will also find these strategies are helpful when addressing specific issues their child may be having with toilet training.

Important Issues

Before you decide to embark on a toilet training mission with your child, you need to give some thought to the following:

Is your child at both a chronological and developmental age where you can reasonably expect her to accept and be able to learn all the facets that toileting consists of?

Interestingly when researching the average age that a typically developed child is ready for toilet training, we found a wide range of ages quoted. Anywhere from 18 months to 32 months were recorded as so-called 'average ages'. However, by far, and in agreement with our own knowledge, around 24 months of age for girls, and slightly older for boys (28 months) would be the average chronological age. Keep in mind if your child is developmentally delayed, she/he may need to be older before she/he is ready for this training. Also remember that every child is different. There is not necessarily a right or wrong age to toilet train. Different cultures also vary with toilet training ages.

Many children with autism may not be fully toilet trained up until they are 4 or even 5 years of age, or older due to developmental considerations and challenges. However, I recommend that at a maximum age to at least attempt a toilet training programme with - for any child disabled or not, is three and a half years of age.

Is your child having longer periods of dry nappies?
If they are now waiting up to 3 hours or so before wetting, that would indicate they have at least some bladder control, and it is likely they can differentiate between a dry nappy (pants) and wet.

Disposables verses cloth nappies
A little to late now to make any changes, however keep in mind that disposable nappies are now very effective in keeping moisture away from babies skin. So, if your child has been wearing only disposables in the months preceding your embarking on toilet training her/him, you may have a slightly tougher time.

Cloth nappies, obviously by the nature of the material, are immediately dampened when a child urinates, and so the child can sense the change from dry to wet, thus aiding their understanding about voiding (toileting). However, do not be dismayed if you have been a firm user of disposables for your children (as the authors have been with most of theirs) all is not lost!

Autism / Intellectual Disability Specific Nappy Issues

One of the most common issues I have come across with the children who have been referred to me is a dependence on nappies that has developed, because it has been allowed to. In some cases the child may have had a good understanding of how to toilet, and even when to toilet, but they had decided that they were more comfortable voiding in their nappy, which in some cases they would even change themself when needed.

When I use the word "comfortable", I don't mean in a "I like the feeling of this" sort of a way. What I mean is, they are comfortable in regards to them having full control (in their mind) of the toileting process. They can go when and where they want, no matter what activity they are involved in at the time. I have found control to be a major factor in many of the behaviours that are sometimes displayed by children with autism. They want to be the one who decides on what, when, how, and where, and unfortunately many of the 'pop-psychologists' and some others seem to go along with this, almost encouraging Parents to ensure they let their child with Autism control everything. Of course, this is setting yourself and your child up for major problems as time goes by!

Some children I have come across will do their wees in the toilet, but insist on doing their poos into a nappy, or even into their pants. There can be many reasons for this, and I discuss this issue more in the 'Desensitisation' chapter of this booklet.

The main point I would like to emphasis at the moment though is, you will probably have to get rid of the nappies completely to make real progress! Yes, this is where many Parents start cursing me, and telling me "That's easy for you to say!", but do not despair, I will talk you through this process more in he different strategies suggested (You will need to trust me).

Potty or toilet?
Please, please, please …… forget using potties! The number of training books and leaflets so called 'child health experts' write, who start off any toilet training advice talking about using a potty, is surprising and a little frightening. I strongly recommend that unless there is a specific physiological reason, or your child is disturbingly terrified of sitting on the toilet, you do not use potties and DO use the toilet itself as the first and only toileting equipment. It makes no sense to spend much time and effort training your child to use a potty, to then only spend more time moving her/him from potty to toilet bowl. For those still not convinced, think it through logically.

Remember when you first learnt to drive, did you spend hours upon hours sitting on a kitchen chair with a toy steering wheel and a wooden spoon gearstick, 'learning' how to drive, or did you start first off in a driving instructor's vehicle (or a brave family member's car)? However, there are toilet seat inserts that make the seat area smaller, so your child feels more comfortable and secure – and doesn't fall down the hole! You can also get mini plastic stools for them to stand on to get on the toilet if needed.

Children with a developmental or intellectual disability in particular will find moving from a potty to a toilet one more confusing step that simply never needed to be there to start with.

Compliance: Is your child currently compliant with most reasonable requests made of him/her?
If your child will come to you when you call, and follow a basic request like "pick up the spoon" or "put the kitten down" on at least 50% of occasions, you can accept your child is at least averagely compliant. This will certainly help the toileting process, as requests to stay on the toilet or to wipe their bottom will be made by you and you will have your and their stress levels greatly reduced if you have reasonable compliance. If you currently have little to no compliance from your child, these strategies will be more difficult to implement. If you feel that your child complies

with little to no requests you make of them, more common with children with moderate or more severe autism and other developmental delays (though not unique to), I suggest you read the chapter included in this booklet about obtaining compliance. ***However, do not rule out toilet training at this time if you feel your child is far from compliant, you may still have success using the strategies supplied as they are designed with the most challenging child in mind.***

Which of the three strategies should you use?

This is really only a question you can answer. The strategies all follow the same basic principles of scheduling (whether it be fixed or to responses observed), and reinforcement. Yet one child may respond quickly to one strategy and not at all to others, where another child may respond to the others but not to that one. I suggest you read through each of them, discuss with your partner or fellow support person, and decide on which one is more likely to succeed taking into account your day-to-day demands of life, and your child's challenges. Though there is no reason you can not try one, and then another if you appear to be having no success, I recommend you give some thought to the one you try first, because if it backfires and turns to disaster this may influence your child's future thinking about using the toilet and make other attempts at training more difficult.

Strategy three ('Sit and wait') is more aimed at children who may be having some trouble with identifying the bladder full sensation or the sensation before a bowel movement. However, if you really can not decide, and feel this really is going to be a mission, I suggest you trial strategy One (the 'Dior Method'), as this uses some extra principles to the other two, that in most cases will see quick success – though a little more energy draining for the parent or support person!

Equipment?
Other than a standard toilet, and maybe a fit-in-toilet seat for toddlers, you need nothing else but lots of patience and a calm demeanour. Remember, I advise against potties.

Strategy One - The 'Dior Method'

This 'Dior Method' relies on your powers of observation, and more importantly on how well you know your child's behaviours, and behavioural cues. That is, being able to recognise what your child usually does just before they void. This may be a certain facial expression, total silence and/or stillness, taking themself to a corner of the room, holding their groin area, a certain movement or posture, etc. If you do not already have an idea of what your child does just before voiding, you will need to carefully observe them over the period of a day or two, taking mental (or written) note of what they did just before they wet or soiled their nappy.

This strategy is one that needs to be run over two or more consecutive days until you have reached success. It is not recommended for just an hour or two now, and another hour later – maybe tomorrow. So plan what two days (maybe more) you will have your child at home with little to no distraction. Preferably days where you do not need to rush off at some stage, and have to put nappies back on your child before you have reached the stage where you want to be that day. In saying that, you can plan for an outing that day as long as you have finished the work for that day (nappy off time) with a success, voiding in the toilet.

Step One

This strategy uses what I call The 'Dior Method'. What this means is, it has had specific strategies added to it that will help the process being learnt. The 'Dior Method' uses scientifically based principles of positive reinforcement, combined with repetition, environmental enhancement and behaviour analysis. Don't let these terms baffle you or concern you, these principles are simply added into the strategy that you are about to read through – and then implement. *(The name 'Dior' just happens to be my youngest daughter's middle name, so nothing mysterious to work out there!)*

You will need to have your child free of their nappies for the day. Obviously if it is not in summertime, you will need to have the house warm by means other than the sun. We want to make the house environment as comfortable as possible. This includes the toilet. **Nothing will put your child off more than a freezing cold loo in a nice warm house!** What I also recommend you now do is add some 'extras' to the toilet room itself. That is, make it attractive to your child. Put one or two posters on the wall that your child loves to look at, maybe a favourite book placed on a string attached to the wall, so it can only be looked at while in the toilet. Ensure the toilet smells nice, even us adults don't like going into a smelly loo! An air freshener will do nicely here, or for a short lasting more child friendly smell, a dab or two of vanilla essence on a small piece of cloth sitting on the windowsill or elsewhere in the toilet will help make the room nicer to visit. Do not fear though – you do not need to keep these 'added extras' there permanently, just for the period of training and for around three to four weeks after the training has been successful.

You now also need to decide on at least two different special reinforcers. These may be special toys that he can play with for three or four minutes after a success, or it may be a special edible treat like three or four M+M's, or similar. The most important thing here is, your child will greatly enjoy this special treat as it is something they usually rarely get. You must also remember that when you do provide this special reinforcer after a success, it must be limited – so they do not get so used to having it they are not interested next time, which is why we say three or four M+M's rather than a pack!

Often children with Autism have a 'special interest' which they love to spend time being involved with. This may be trains, dinosaurs, a certain TV show, etc. If you can obtain an item that relates to this special interest, that they have not had access to in the past, this would be a great item that they only get access to when they have just toileted in the toilet, and they do not get access to it at any other time. Also limit the time they get to interact with or look at the item (no more than a minute), or again it will lose it's value to your child.

Other than having the child's nappy removed, do not drastically change the rest of the normal daily routine, other than you are suddenly taking an even bigger interest in watching them play than usual.

Step Two
Monitor your child every minute. As soon as it appears they are about to void, pick them up gently but quickly and walk with them straight to the toilet. While holding them, and in those few seconds it takes for you to reach them and pick them up, say "Wait, wait, wait*......" and continue this until after having placed them on the toilet itself. If any of the urine or bowel motion actually does go into the bowl (which is the main goal of course) make a really big deal about it. "Great, fantastic, what a good girl/boy, well done"! Lots of hugs and smiles, and have that special reinforcer available right then and there. **It is very important you provide that special reinforcer almost immediately, so they connect the positive behaviour (voiding in the toilet) with a positive event afterwards (access to that special toy, the special snack, etc).** Though your child may not understand what 'wait' means at this time, in most cases they will soon connect the word 'wait' with the message you are trying to get across.

If by the time you reach the toilet, they have already voided (yes, unfortunately this may happen – and most likely more than once), still sit them on the toilet for at least two minutes. It is important your child relates voiding with sitting on the toilet. This will also help them get used to sitting on the toilet.

Do not tell them off if they have already voided before reaching the toilet. You can however say, "Nearly made it, next time you will make it". Be calm, though this is hard when you may have a mess to clean up, it is important as your child will pick up on any negative comments, facial expressions, or movements you make and this may make them think of the toilet as a scary negative place. Unfortunately you do not let them have the special reinforcer if they did not void into the toilet, but do not make a big deal about this (i.e. do NOT say "you can't have your treat now", as this will just start to create stress around the whole issue of toileting, and create more of a challenge).

Of course some children with a developmental or intellectual disability may not be able to understand or process many words at once. So, you can just use key words which if they do not understand straight away, they will probably learn the general meaning of over time. For example just saying "Never mind" in a calm tone with low volume is fine if they have an accident.

Step Three
Eventually you should see your child start moving towards the toilet themselves when they need to void, and you need only take their hand and calmly but quickly walk with them (not pull them) to the toilet, and assist them when there - if needed.

Step Four
Once your child has voided successfully four times in succession (all in the toilet bowl), they can now 'graduate' to wearing undies. Keep in mind though, even though they are now in undies rather than nappies, you may need to keep repeating step one, two and three until you have more dry times than wet. Remember to get them to pull their pants down by themselves once in the toilet, though you may need to help them a little the first one or two times. Also cue them to wipe their bottom, pull pants up, and flush the toilet by themself (where physically possible of course). Again remember the 'well done, fantastic,' comments and the special reinforcer access. **However, it is also now time to start fading the reinforcers**. Start with the special reinforcer, only presenting it for access maybe every second occasion, then every third, then either at random, or stop completely. If your child is not able to do these tasks (pulling pants down, wiping, pants up, etc), provide some hand-over-hand prompting and fade as time progresses

One common problem I have also come across over the years around toilet training and children with autism, is that they sometimes have mastered most of the toilet training process, except two or three steps which they still insist their Parents do for them. More often than not those steps are around wiping their bottoms and flushing the toilet.

I do not want to sound harsh, but often those particular problems have started and continued (sometimes for months or even years!), because their Parents have let them do so. Now in saying this, I am sure in 99% of the cases I have come across the Parents have not intended on this happening, but they allow it to continue when they really do not need to.

To help prevent this problem, always prompt your child to not just void in the toilet, as per strategy, but to also do all the other needed steps, wiping themselves, putting the toilet paper in the bowl, flushing the toilet, pulling their pants back up, then washing their hands. If you do need to use hand over hand prompting to start with, then do so, but slowly fade it out as you can over the next few days or weeks (depending on the ability and speed of your child to learn these new skills).

Step Five
Remember to generalise. Once your child has achieved success in reaching the 'underwear on' stage, start exposing

them to other environments (fully clothed obviously!). For example - shopping malls, libraries, houses of friends and family. When arriving, show your child where the toilet is there. The first two or three visits to each location you may need to monitor them fairly closely to watch for behaviour that suggests they may need to void soon, if so, prompt them to go to the toilet. Even at a friend's house, support them by going with them the first two or three times, remember new toilet – added stress.

Many children with autism or Aspergers find using another toilet very stressful, as it is different from the routine and environment they were used to. It may be helpful before going to another environment where you will want your child t use the toilet there, to tell them before you go, in simple terms "We are going to * * * * * *, there will be a toilet there, you will use that toilet." I believe that a big part of the support process for children and adults with autism is to always ensure they know what is going on, and the basics of what will be expected of them.

Again, remember to give lots of positive verbal reinforcement in the new environment, so they know you are pleased when they use other toilets as well as the one at home. Try and share the training between support people as well. For example: your partner, other caregivers, grandparents, older siblings, etc. It is important that your child toilets for others and not just you.

WHAT IF ...

"I just can't work out the cues, she/he just seems to go wee whenever and wherever"
Then you need to see if your partner, or other caregivers have noticed any specific little behaviour that she/he does before voiding. It may even be as simple as making eye contact, or avoiding eye contact. If you really can't find those cues though, you will be better off trying one of the other two strategies.

"He gets really upset when I pick him up and take him to the toilet"
Unfortunately you just need to work through this one. Same old story, ignore the unwanted behaviour – positively reinforce the wanted behaviour. However, ensure you are not frightening your child by the way you are picking them up and rushing them there. Though you do need to act quickly, to avoid a mess and increase chances of success, if it becomes a very frightening experience this could well achieve the opposite of what you want. That is, your child becomes terrified of the bladder/bowel–full feeling, and of going to the toilet! Try making it a fun experience, singing a favourite song or nursery rhyme on the way to the toilet is one method, rather than using the 'wait, wait' prompt. Remember though; as you get some success start fade this singing or game-play, or your child may expect this to

happen every time as it is now part of their 'set toileting routine'

Strategy Two – Sit and Wait

This strategy can see toilet training completed within one to two days, even with many children who have a moderate to severe developmental delay. Yet it takes much patience by both you and your child! It may also be somewhat stressful for you both, though shared between two to three people – it will not take to much of a toll on you, and if your child is supplied with enough toys, books, etc (as detailed below) it should not be too stressful for them either.

Step One
Set up a seat in, or at the door, of the toilet. This seat is for you, or the caregiver talking their turn supporting your child. Also place in or just at the door a box of favourite toys, books, puzzles, etc (no not yours, your child's!). Also have handy (though not in the toilet area yet) a seat for your child, for him/her to sit on a little further along in the process.

Step Two
Immediately after having breakfast, including a drink, sit your child on the toilet, with you sitting on your seat near them. Obviously, do not have him/her wearing nappies or pants during this process. **Give him a toy or book to play with, and encourage him to stay on the toilet seat. As soon as she/he voids, provide those great verbal**

reinforcements immediately "Great, fantastic, what a good boy, well done, you did wee/poo in the toilet that's so good"! Help him wipe himself if needed, and now put undies on him (yes, straight into undies with this strategy, no nappies at the moment. You can now also give him a fifteen-minute reprieve from sitting on the toilet. Let him go and do whatever he wishes to. However, in the last five minutes, prompt him again to have a drink (preferably at least half a glass). Provide whatever needed to ensure he will drink it, yes even the dreaded soft drink - just for this exercise. After the fifteen-minute break – you guessed it, back to sitting on the toilet. They need to sit there until they void again, then repeat the process again, fifteen-minute break, drink, etc.

Step Three
Once the child has voided at least five times, on the sixth session, place them on a chair next to the toilet seat. Watch for cues that they may be about to void, or if they start voiding on the chair itself, quickly but calmly lift them onto the toilet bowl (hopefully, she will get up off the seat and get onto the toilet unprompted and void in there). If over 50% of the void goes into the bowl, again provide the positive reinforcers and the fifteen-minute break. If most goes on the seat or floor, clean them up – say nothing, and sit them back down on their seat, do not appear or act angry or upset, but at the same time do not make eye contact or say anything for at least a minute or two (though if they are

overly upset, it is ok to calm them as you need to, but make this as short as possible). You may now need to provide another drink to initiate more urination. If you have more than three 'misses' in a row, go back to step one – sitting them on the actual toilet until they void in there. Wait again until you get two voids in the bowl, then back to sitting on the seat, repeating this step again.

Step Four
When you have achieved two successes, with your child getting up off the seat to void in the toilet bowl, move the seat about four feet (just over a metre) away from the toilet bowl, and continue the sessions – **breaks after successful voids can now be thirty minutes long.** Each time you have a success, move the seat (and yours) another four feet away from the toilet. You should now also be prompting him to wipe himself, and pull pants up by himself (use hand-over-hand prompting if needed). When you (and your child) are really achieving great things – with her chair around twenty feet from the toilet, increase the breaks from thirty to around forty minutes, again with a drink in those last few minutes.

Step Five
Once you are over the twenty feet mark, simply loose the chair altogether, and simply provide a verbal prompt about every forty minutes for "toilet time", you may need to take

her hand and lead her there for the first one or two times, just to get her used to walking there from any part of the house, rather than just from the chair she was on. Continue with the verbal reinforcement, but slowly fading it now.

You should now have a nearly toilet-trained child! However, yes things may not run as smooth as we would want, and you may have to run the sessions over a period of two days or more until you get to the desired level of consistency of voiding in the toilet. If you are not having any success with your child self-initiating sitting on the toilet to void, from the seat you have placed them on, after say five attempts on the chair, and you have gone back to step one before trying the second step again, have a break for say two hours, then return again to step one and start over. Yes, you do need lots of patience!

If your child is becoming extremely anxious over sitting on the toilet bowl right from the first session of an extended period of time, despite your attempts to amuse her with toys and books from the box you have, you may need to try a desensitisation process with the toilet to start with (see desensitising notes later in this booklet). **Once the desensitising process is finished, then come back to this strategy.**

WHAT IF …

'After ten minutes he is sick of sitting on the toilet, and tantrums to such a degree I can not get him to stay there'
This is tough, though we really need them to stay on until success (and you should work through this if you can), we also do not want the experience of being on the toilet to be a negative on. If your best attempts to engage them in what you have there for them fails, let them go to where they want to go. However, do not let them have access to other items they want that are not in the toilet (i.e. watching TV, playing on the playground, etc). **If the things outside of the toilet are so much more fun, and they can access them just by tantruming, they will do it again and again.** While they are settling down, reassess what items you have there in the toilet area that will be of interest, are they really his favourite things? Is there a game you can play while he sits there, nursery rhymes to sing, photo albums to look through, etc? Once you have found some more interesting and 'exciting' activities, and he has calmed right down, try again.

If still tantruming to such a degree you have to let him go again, this time – once he is calm, 'prime him' with lots and lots of drinks! Once he can't get another drop down*, take him to the toilet again, and this time insist he stays there, nature will quickly take its course and he will urinate in the bowl while there, even if tantruming at the time. But that's ok – you have had a success! Provide the verbal reinforcement, special reinforcers, and let him have his break. He now knows, weeing in the loo equals nice things. Next time, the tantrums should be less, if not, again repeat what I have just suggested.

Do be sensible with the 'lots of drinks' advice, you do not want to cause your child any physical harm. That is, don't force the drinks down, let them drink freely – this is why, as suggested earlier in this chapter, you may need to forgo your rules about no fizzy drinks or juices so he is more than happy to drink lots of his favourites, just until we get this toileting under control.

Strategy Three – Fixed Scheduling

This is maybe the most energy draining of the three strategies suggested in this book. However, if you feel the other two strategies are unlikely to be suitable for your child, or what you can realistically cope with, this may be the one to try. It may also be an option if you have given one or both the others a try, and had little to no success

Step One
Set a day or two aside where you will have little to no interruption in regards to appointments, etc. You need to decide on a set timeframe for taking your child to the toilet for the first part of this strategy. That is, every 20 minutes, 30 minutes, or 40 minutes. I suggest 20, but definitely no more than 40 minutes between toilet trips. One thing you need to take into consideration around this is how often your child usually wets or poos in her nappy, if it is very regular, the shorter time span of 20 minutes would be better, if it is only 2 – 3 times per day, the 40 minutes may be the better option. Either way, the whole goal of this strategy is to get your child into the habit of going to the toilet from whatever room they are in, and to interrupt whatever it is she/he is doing to go to the toilet instead of going in their nappy.

Step Two

At the time you have decided on (lets say you start the exercise at 9am, and decided on 20 minute intervals) **pick your child up, simply say "toilet time" and have no other interaction with her.** Once in the toilet, remove the nappy and place her on the toilet seat. Stay with her there for at least four minutes (this doesn't sound that long, but it will seem like a lifetime once you start this exercise!). If she gets off the toilet, simply place her back on as gently and calmly as you can, not having any other verbal interaction with her. At the end of the four minutes, get her off the toilet, say "Good girl" (or boy - accordingly) put her nappy back on, and let her make her own way back to what she/he was doing. If she/he voids while on the toilet seat, ensure you immediately provide her with lots of verbal reinforcement - "Great, fantastic, what a good girl, well done, you did wee/poo in the toilet - that's so good"! Give her a hug, and then finish the process - wiping and flushing (let her help with this if possible – but do not force her). Now also provide a special reinforcer, this may be a special video or music CD, favourite game, etc (as discussed earlier in this chapter). **It is important you provide this special reinforcer immediately after the success, to connect the special 'treat' with the good appropriate behaviour.**

Step Three
Continue as above. When/if you have success with her voiding in the toilet bowl twice, now try her with just undies on – loose the nappy. Also now change from carrying her to the toilet, to leading her by her hand.

Step Four
After another two successes, instead of leading her by her hand, just use the verbal prompt of "Toilet time", and walk there with her.

Step Five
After one more success, now increase your time spans by 10 minutes, but obviously if your child prompts you that she/he needs to go – by either making her way there by herself, or saying "Toilet time" go with her at that time, do not try and wait until the time period is up. Now simply let things take their course. That is, slowly increase the time spans (little by little) until you feel comfortable she/he can/does now go to the toilet under her own steam, or prompts you to let you know she/he needs to go. **Guard against her becoming reliant on you always accompanying her, start going only to the toilet door, then to just before the toilet door, and so on until she/he is comfortable going the whole way by herself.** Again remember to generalise and have your partner or other caregivers take turns in following through the strategy. If

you have more than one toilet at home, alternate between them so she/he is not reliant on just one toilet for going in, and this will help her to adjust to using toilets in other environments.

WHAT IF ...

'She keeps weeing in her nappy, and after a whole day of following this strategy we have had no successes at all!'
That's ok! But what it does mean is that you need to repeat the process again the next day, and maybe the next – until you get those successes!. **Until you get that first and often second success, your child may not understand what it is they are supposed to be doing on the toilet, nor will they experience the positive reinforcers that you are going to provide once she/he does void in the toilet.** So, to help with this, on day two now provide a drink five minutes before the time period ends. That is, if you are using 20 minute time periods (and you should be using the shorter ones now if you had no success with longer time spans) then provide a drink after about 15 minutes. Also, increase the time sitting on the toilet to six minutes.

'If still no successes?"
If still no successes after two (by now very tiring) days, have a one-day break. When trying the third day, follow the suggestions as above, but this time keep her on the toilet until she/he does void. Have a book or toy there she/he can play with to help pass the time, and lessen the chances of boredom and resulting tantrums.

'We had two successes, but now I have tried her with underwear she is getting really upset and refusing to wear

them, she wants the nappies back even though she is weeing in the loo'

Time to be tough, and do what many Parents dread about now – get rid of the nappies 100% (Though you can still have them in one for sleep time only at this stage). Many children with autism appear to be confused when allowed to still wear nappies though also using the toilet. After all nappies are for doing wees and poos into', so why would I wear those and also be expected to do my wees and poos into the loo? Makes no sense at all! Trust me, if you now give in and let them wear nappies, usually you will go backwards in what you have achieved to date.

Night Time TIPs

The biggest factor in achieving night time success (either a dry night, or your child waking and appropriately toileting with little to no support) is firstly achieving day time success. That is, when they are using the toilet with little to no prompting during the day, the night time with eventually come right. However, sometimes nights do become yet another obstacle to overcome in the toilet training drama. So, here are some tips that may make things a little easier:

The Basics: There are some very basic things that will help with nights.

- **Firstly, no drinks within 90 minutes of bedtime.** (This can be really difficult, as many children are in the habit of having a bedtime drink, and especially with children with autism, breaking this long held routine can be quite traumatic. If so, instead of ruling out all drinks in that 90 minutes before bed, just allow very small drinks, maybe one about 90 minutes out of say a third of a glass, then another just before bed – but no more than a quarter of a glass. Over the next few nights, slowly reduce these amounts even more until it is just a couple of sips before toilet then bed.

- **Always ensure they go to toilet immediately before going to bed.** This is an important habit to form. Not only does it give them that last opportunity to void before bedtime, it also helps keep 'using the toilet' fresh in their minds if they do wake at night needing to go, rather than going in bed which was the habit they used to have.

- **Do NOT put any pressure on them to "have a dry night".** If you make a big fuss about this, they will worry all night long – stress will increase the likelihood of them wetting the bed.

- **When there is an 'accident' (a wet bed) again, do NOT make a fuss about it.** Do not tell them off, do not tell them you are sad about it, nothing. Instead just clean it up in a low key manner.

One Step at a Time – Night Toileting Strategy

Remember this 'toilet thing' is a new experience, and just learning the daytime routine has been a big trial for your child. So when it comes to night-time toileting don't expect miracles the first two or three nights.

On the first night, put your child to bed in underwear rather than a nappy. However, you are going to wake them up after three hours, and prompt them to go to the toilet. Yes, they will be grumpy and you will be in the bad books. Once they get to the toilet, ensure they sit on the bowl for at least a minute – even if they do not void. Do not keep them much longer than a minute though – again we do not want to make the toileting experience a bad one. When they get back to their room, you can put their nappy back on for the night (If you want to try the rest of the night in undies, that is fine too – but again, do not expect a miracle). Repeat this three more nights, and then the next three stretch it out to three and a half hours before toileting. What you have now achieved is your child is used to going to bed in undies and getting up to go toilet from their bed. You can now attempt the first night in undies

There are products to help: Unfortunately it is likely you will have some wet beds, and you will cringe at the thought of yet more bedclothes to wash! But there are some products that will help you get through this faze. You can get plastic or rubber under-sheets that stop the moisture soaking through into the mattress.

WHAT IF ...

"I have tried and tried what you have suggested, but she/he still keeps wetting her nappy at night time".
Again look at how much your child is drinking leading up to bedtime. Remember, no drinks within 90 minutes of bedtime, and before this, frequent small drinks would be better than two or three large ones.

"I've done that, but still wet nappies"!
Ok. You will need to do the long yards I'm afraid. Night one – put your child to bed in undies, as the original strategy advises. Wake her after two hours, toilet. Wake her another two hours, toilet. Then three hours time, toilet. That should be enough for the night. Repeat this for one more night. The third night, wake her every three hours for toileting. Next night, wake once after three hours, leave her in nappies. Keep this up for at least another three or four nights. Now, again try for a full night – in undies. If still no success (or at least if no more successes than failures), then seek medical advice as your child may possibly have a bladder problem. This may not be the case, but always check it out. If there is no medical problem, again go back to trying the original strategy, remembering all the 'basic tips'.

"The biggest factor in achieving night time success is firstly achieving day time success"

Poo's In The Loo

A problem I have come across several times over the years is children with autism who will do all their wees into the toilet without a problem, but will either not poo at all into a toilet, or only selective toilets, often only the home one. If this is the problem you are trying to tackle, there are a few things you need to look at before you proceed with a strategy taken from my suggestions in the rest of this section.

First of all you need to work out what is the exact reason your child will not do their poos into the toilet, or into some other toilets. The reasons can be many, but the more commons issues are usually:

- **Already in the habit of doing poos elsewhere.** That is, they have been doing their poos into a nappy or pants (or elsewhere) for so long it is now 'just what they do'. This is a common problem with people with autism, once something is done a certain way for a long period of time, it can be very difficult convincing them that actually – you should do this, not that.

- **Don't like the feeling of a cold toilet seat on their bottom.** Sensory issues are of course fairly common with children who have autism. Most of us are not that happy with a cold or uncomfortable toilet seat, but when you are extra sensitive to touch, this can be an even bigger problem.

- **The 'Splash' issue.** Some children have done poo's into the toilet once or twice, and then stopped wanting to do them again. Sometimes his is due to them experiencing the 'splash' of toilet water as they did a poo. It obviously made them uncomfortable or even gave them a fright. Remember, what happens immediately after a behaviour is what determines the likelihood of that behaviour being repeated in the future.

- **Control – "Where do my poos go?"** As many parents with a child with autism will know, one of the constant issues you face is your child's want to 'control' as much of life as they can. Sometimes that 'want' means they need to know how things work, and in the case of toileting "Where does my poo go after it goes into the bowl?"

Unfortunately working out which of the above possible issues may be impacting your child's toileting is not always easy. But, you can take some steps to help rule out or solve each of these without those steps negatively affecting the toileting process in general. Below are some basic strategies that you can implement to help solve the issues mentioned.

Habit: *If it is a certain time that your child is doing his/her poos somewhere rather than the toilet, then about 15 minutes before that time is due is the time to take them to the toilet, and prompt them to do their poos there. You should work this in, in conjunction with the main strategies described where possible, however the main thing we want to achieve here is to break the current habit. Breaking a habit is usually successful when we introduce a new habit, particularly if it is incompatible with the current habit. So with this issue, it is all about having them on the toilet around the time they usually do their poos in their pants, nappy, or other. It may also be that you need to get rid of the nappies altogether, if that is what they are doing their poos into. Or, if it is in a certain pair of pants, but slightly different ones, as well as following the toilet time advice.*

Cold Toilet Seat: *This is a more difficult one, however there are some things that may help. You may want to introduce a routine to your child where they can wipe the toilet seat round and round say five or six times before sitting on it to warm it up a little. There are also some cloth type toilet seat warmers you may be able to use on the toilet to keep the seat warmer.*

Splash: *Have your child put a handful of toilet paper into the bowl first, this will eliminate or reduce the 'splash' issue.*

"Where do my poo's go?" *A basis visual or even a social story can help explain where the poos go, from bowl to sewer pipe to sewer, to the treatment process. This seems like a lot of work to do for what you may think is just silly, but to your child it may be very important, and they may feel a lot more comfortable with the 'poos in the loo' when they know what happens to them.*

ROUTINE and HABIT

Passing bowel motions usually follows a specific routine in regards to when the bowel motion occurs. This routine becomes more regular with age, and is not quite so regular when we are very young. However, you should find that your child often does have a bowel motion (BM) during a certain time period of the day or night. This might be between 9am and 11am, or 6pm and 8pm. Whenever it is, you need to be watching your child extra closely so you can pick up any signs that they may be about to have a BM, so the next time they show those signs you can take them straight to the toilet and sit them on it hopefully to get them to have the BM then and there. The more they associate that feeling of about to have a bowel motion and then sitting on the toilet, the more likely they will start doing this without your prompts.

WHAT DOES IT FEEL LIKE WHEN I NEED TO 'POO'?

One issue with BM's is that they feel different from having a 'wee'. That is, the physical sensations that your child now recognises as meaning they need to wee are different from those for when they need to 'poo'. When you can get that first BM in the toilet, you are on your way to getting more BMs in there. Just like the weeing, as your child learns to associate the physical sensations of having a full bowel with sitting on the toilet, they will start to self-initiate that behaviour.

ISN'T THAT WHAT NAPPIES ARE FOR?

Many parents keep using nappies even though their child has now mastered the urination side of toileting, in case they 'have an accident'. But to a child, the fact they are still wearing nappies may be a little confusing. In other words, now that they wee in the toilet, why do they still have this nappy thing on? Maybe because that is what you do your poos in?

You will need to try and get out of the habit of using nappies (including 'Pull Ups') as soon as possible after your child has mainly successes with 'weeing' in the toilet.

Though you may still want a nappy on occasions if you are going out somewhere and they still have the odd accident, at home try to be completely nappy-free. This in itself will help aid your child to understand that everything that comes out below belongs only in the loo.

GAMES ARE GOOD

Doing poos is not a fun experience for many kids. All that pushing while sitting over a big hole can be scary. Bowel motions can also cause some discomfort and even pain, so the thought of sitting on the toilet doing the poos can be daunting to a small child.

To help ease some of this possible anxiety, make a game out of 'poo's in the loo'

For example, have a colour-in picture on the toilet wall. Each time your child does do a poo in the loo they get to colour in a part of the picture. When the picture is all coloured in, they get a 'prize'. Of course again you want to reinforce the BM in the toilet behaviour straight away, and make it quick and easy to get the reinforcement. So, especially the first two or three times they get their BM in the toilet, give them a special treat straight away. Remember to also tell them how happy and pleased you are with them.

DON'T PUNISH FOR ACCIDENTS

If you growl your child when they do have a BM in their nappy or pants (or dare I say it – somewhere else), don't be angry with them. In fact don't make a fuss one way or the other. Simply clean it up, don't say anything about what happened, and once all is cleaned up – you can simply say (in a non sarcastic manner) "Never mind, next time we will get the 'poo in the loo'."

If you tell them off, or make them feel unhappy or uncomfortable about what happened, next time they may be even more secretive about it, not wanting you to know. They may even associate the act of having a BM as being bad altogether, and so even going to the toilet won't be an option, because 'Mum will know and I'll get told off again'.

Desensitisation

"Mummy, I really don't like wearing undies!"
Some children have difficulty going from nappies to undies. This is particularly common with children who have autism, and is also seen with some other developmentally delayed and intellectually disabled children. Don't get distressed about this, there is a solution.

Guidelines for desensitising your child to wearing undies:
Get your child involved in the undies choosing exercise. That is, when you go out to buy some, take them with you – let them select the colour/pattern that they like. At this stage you do not want to frighten or stress them, so you do not need to even say things like "These are what you will be wearing", simply say, something like "Look at these pretty pants – which ones do you think are the nicest?". Yes, it's true that some children may not have the interaction or choosing skills at this stage to have much input here, and in some cases you may have already bought the undies, or your child may not be at a level where they can participate in this sort of exercise. However, where possible, do follow this step prior to implementing the toilet training.

I would also like to acknowledge that for some Parents who have a child with autism, going into a store and going through this process may be a little too daunting sometimes. If this is the case at the moment, buy three or four different patterns / types, then present them to your child and ask the same question. Again you are letting them have some control and choice over what it is they will be wearing, increasing the likelihood of them being happy to wear them, but you are avoiding the whole in the shop' stress.

Don't just shove them straight on. Going from wearing the same thing day after day all your life (well, your life to date) to something that looks different, feels different, and is all about NOT weeing or pooing in, can naturally be frightening or at least stressful for many children. What you need to do is let them get used to the idea, slowly. This is what we call desensitising.

Let your child get used to what they look like. Let them get used to what they look like. Leave them on a chair or on the dresser in their room for a day or two.

Let them feel what they are like to touch. Remember, this is a different type of material from what they are used to having against their skin. Create opportunities where they can pick them up, and hold them. Play a game where you sit the undies on their knee, see how well they can fold them up, and so on. Anything that involves them getting used to the feel of them is great.

The process of following the previous steps may take a few days to implement, particularly if your child is reacting in a negative way to the wearing of underpants.

"No Way am I sitting on That Seat with the Big Hole in it!"
Some children are terrified of toilets right from the start! They are worried about falling through the hole, the seat is freezing cold, they feel insecure, the toilet is small and frightening, or it's just that it is something so different to everything else they do. To help combat your child's fear of sitting on the toilet, you may need to desensitise them to the experience before embarking on the strategies of toilet training.

Get them used to the toilet area. Play games outside the toilet area, in the hallway. Have the toilet door open, occasionally let a ball or toy roll in there so your child needs to go in there and retrieve it. (yes hygiene is a concern, but I am sure you will have mopped and cleaned in there before going to this step!).

Ensure the toilet is a nice place to visit. Is it clean? Does it smell nice? Buy a poster or two that your child will love to look at, involve them in the process of sticking these on the toilet walls (blue tack will do nicely here). Have them positioned so you actually need to enter the toilet room to see them properly. Ensure there is an air freshener or similar in there. Maybe a novelty ornament on the windowsill may also be helpful.

Get them used to the sensation of sitting on a seat with a hole. There are a few ways you can achieve this. One, if you see a cheap toilet seat for sale – great, buy it. Then play a game where the toilet seat sits on the sofa or another chair, and your child has to sit on the seat (ensure this is a fun exercise though, don't frighten them with the seat!). As there is no hole as such at this time, they shouldn't have too much of a concern about it.

Another possibility is, if you have an old plastic chair (like the plastic garden chairs), carefully cut out a small hole in the middle of the seat area (only about 5 cm's wide at this stage), encourage your child to sit on this seat, again use it as part of a game, or when they have their lunch maybe this is the chair they sit on – just for now. Each day, for the next five days, cut about an extra centimetre around the hole, so by the fifth day the hole is now around 10cms across. Have them sit on the seat say two more times, before going into the toilet training strategy.

Gaining Compliance

Gaining compliance from your child is sometimes more about regaining control over their behaviour. I have found time and time again some children, usually with autism, want to be the one in control of almost all situations. This means they are unlikely to follow most requests as they want to be the one deciding what they will and won't do, not you.

Whether your child has Autism, another disability, or no disability at all, the fact you are their Parents does not change. Part of being a successful Parent is being in control of what your child does and does not do. Now having been a parent of four children myself, I am well aware how easy that sounds and how very, very difficult it is to achieve in reality!

However, there are some ways of regaining that control, and gaining compliance to reasonable requests while at the same time teaching our children they do have choices in life where they can make the decision about what happens, while accepting the possible consequences of their choice.

Choices
One way of gaining and keeping control is by presenting choices, so your child still feels that they have some control but learn to understand ultimately you have the overriding

control of their behaviour in most situations. For example if your child had been given two chocolate bars as a gift, you could say *"You can eat one before 4 o'clock today, and one after breakfast tomorrow. Or, you can eat both tomorrow straight after breakfast". Now your child can choose which one they prefer, but notice how eating them before dinner or before bed is not an option. If they go back to wanting to do that, you simply present the choices again. If they persist, or attempt to eat them now anyway, this is where you get tough (yes that is part of being a parent, sometimes being the 'bad guy' or girl) and remove the chocolate bars, and again tell them they can have them either after breakfast tomorrow, end if discussion. Yes, they can scream and rant and rave as much as they like, but you have now made the decision for them, and you have shown ultimately you are in control.

*Note: Children with autism will often find instructions easier to understand if you communicate them in clear simple steps, trying to give enough time to process each step (even if just a few seconds) before giving the next step.

Consistency and Following Through
Having consistency is also an important part of gaining compliance for reasonable requests from your child. If one day you let them get away with leaving their toys all over the floor, and just tidy them up yourself, yet the next day prompt them that they "Must pick up after yourself", your

child is learning that actually, no they don't always need to pick up after themselves because just yesterday you did it, without a problem. So they start to question whether you really mean what you say, and whether they can sometimes do what they like, by just holding out a little more.

Children with autism, as I am sure you will know, follow rules to the highest extent possible, once they understand what the rule is and accept it. This also means they expect everyone else to also follow that same rule, and often it isn't far off World War Three if someone breaks a rule, especially one that they always stick to. This means you need to be consistent with everyone, if you have a rule about picking up after yourself; this also has to apply to siblings and even Mum and Dad!

If you have explained choices and consequences, you must ensure you follow through every time. For example if the positive consequence for picking up the toys when finished was to be allowed a milkshake, then don't go changing things once the toys are picked up. For example "Well, yes you can have a milkshake, but you will have to wait until after dinner now." Remember most people, and especially those who have autism, don' like to have a promise broken, or a consequence or condition suddenly changed at the whim of the person who explained the consequences.

If you fail to follow through, firstly your child will lose faith in you and you will struggle to get them to believe you or even listen to you in the future. Secondly you are creating confusion for your child. Most people with autism are very 'concrete' with their thinking, and if you have told them 'this is what happens afterwards' and then it doesn't happen, they will usually become either quite angry and upset, or will isolate themselves, trying to process why what they expected to happen did not happen.

SUMMARY

In summary, I have to say what Parents sometimes find hard to accept when they may have struggled for months or even years to get their child toilet trained. "Don't over think it, don't complicate it. Toilet training is often an easier process than what you think it is"

'Do-Gooders' and even sometimes 'Professionals' are not necessarily of any real help to many parents trying to toilet train a child with autism or intellectual disability, nor may they even be allies to the process. But, confidence, and consistency are your two main allies here. Welcome them, embrace them, and use them without any doubt in your mind that they will be a large part of successful toilet training.

I have at times even said to Parents "Forget everything you have been told about toilet training, start again from the beginning like you are only just embarking on the process." I then explain my strategies, as outlined in this booklet, and reinforce the importance of consistency and confidence, and persistence is important too.

Don't give up because the toilet training doesn't go well one day, or even a couple of days in a row. Instead, reread the strategies if needed, and rethink your whole approach and attitude to what you want to achieve.

Good luck, *you can do it!*

Trevor Lewis

You may also find my other books and booklets helpful in modifying unwanted behaviour, teaching social skills, managing anger, etc. You can find these other resources on my website:
www.behaviourskills.com

Important Toilet Training Note

The strategies listed in this booklet, though designed mainly for children with autism, or another developmental disability, they are fairly general and non-specific to any one individual. Some children, particularly those who display very challenging behaviour or have a severe to profound intellectual or developmental disability may require a custom designed toilet training strategy, or the assistance of trained therapists. However, we recommend you trial the strategies as outlined in the booklet, and do not give up easily, as they have been successful in training even severely intellectually disabled children, and children greatly affected by autism in a relatively short period of time.

If your child appears to be retaining faeces, or not voiding their bladder at a rate you think is needed to be healthy, please do talk things through with your GP, and do not be afraid to push for a full assessment by a specialist. Sometimes it can be a medical problem affecting the toilet training process, so don't be talked out of having a full medical assessment to rule this out, or to provide treatment if something is found amiss.

The author does not make any guarantees that the strategies will be successful, nor can he take responsibility for any unwanted results. Though the author has used specialist knowledge in designing these strategies, those who follow them take all care and responsibility themselves for all and any outcome.

Image by Emma Lewis

Made in the USA
Lexington, KY
18 January 2015